The Santa Claus Project

The Santa Claus Project

Stories of discovery
about
a man in a red suit

Edited
by
Marsha and Matt Schmidt

authorHOUSE®

AuthorHouse™
1663 Liberty Drive
Bloomington, IN 47403
www.authorhouse.com
Phone: 1-800-839-8640

Published by AuthorHouse   09/25/2012

ISBN: 978-1-4772-6777-6 (sc)
ISBN: 978-1-4772-6776-9 (e)

Library of Congress Control Number: 2012916766

Any people depicted in stock imagery provided by Thinkstock are models, and such images are being used for illustrative purposes only.
Certain stock imagery © Thinkstock.

This book is printed on acid-free paper.

Because of the dynamic nature of the Internet, any web addresses or links contained in this book may have changed since publication and may no longer be valid. The views expressed in this work are solely those of the author and do not necessarily reflect the views of the publisher, and the publisher hereby disclaims any responsibility for them.

TABLE OF CONTENTS

Foreword

When we first began thinking about creating this book, we thought we would be reading a lot of stories about childhood discoveries and disappointments. We were surprised to find that stories about Santa Claus tell us a lot about culture and society, times and places, and family mores and traditions. We learned what it was like to grow up in cities, small towns, and farms. We learned about Santa in department stores, and Santa playing a banjo. The stories show that even as generations pass, and visions of Santa might change, the innocence of a child never does.

Kids are pretty smart despite the elaborate ruses concocted by parents. But it is the eyes of Santa that matter most. It always seems to be the eyes that have helped a child make that differentiation between Santa and the man they know, be it a father or a friend, who was pretending to be Santa.

We hope you enjoy reading these stories as much as we did. Take a trip back to your own childhood and the days when Santa was real and the anticipation interminable.

Introduction

The Santa Claus Myth
by
Marsha K. Schmidt

I have always been interested in the psychology of the Santa Claus myth. What is the impact on a child when they learn the truth? What happens to that wide-eyed excitement of a child and the innocent belief in the goodness of a man in a red suit? Having perpetuated the myth with our own little deceptions, are we teaching them that adults can't be trusted? Is their first lesson in life one of disillusionment and disappointment? Are we teaching them that life is actually not as nice as we assured them it would be and that hopes and dreams are just an illusion? What does this really do to kids?

It turns out that kids are pretty resilient. Based on a few studies,[1] researchers have

---

[1] Anderson, C., Prentice, N., *Encounter with Reality: Children's Reactions on Discovering the Santa Claus Myth*, 25 Child Psychiatry and Human Development 1994 Winter 25(2):67-84; Prentice, N., Schmechel, L., Manosevitz, M., *Children's Belief in Santa Claus: A Developmental Study of Fantasy and Causality*, Journal of the American Academy of Child Psychiatry 1979 Jan., 18(4): 658-667; *Santa Claus: Good or Bad for Children?* Journal of Pediatric Health Care (1996). 10, 243-244; Vines, G., *The Santa Claus Delusion: is it harmless fantasy*

found that kids cope just fine with the truth. It all comes down to the flying reindeer and the chimney. Small children have not yet learned to distinguish between fantasy and reality. They will readily believe in flying reindeer and the magic of a man who can jump down a chimney. Parents perpetuate and encourage these beliefs with seemingly plausible explanations and by leaving evidence such as empty milk glasses and crumbs left on a plate.

But as a child gets a little older, around six or seven, they start to see that this cannot be reality and they develop doubts. How can reindeer fly? Birds fly. Planes fly. But reindeer? Chimneys are small and some houses don't even have chimneys. As they start to put it together, they can see that it cannot possibly be true. Mom and dad try to keep up the myth but eventually the kids start asking questions. Why does Santa's handwriting look like your handwriting? Why are there so many Santas? Why does Santa look like Uncle Mike? After a few timid tries, or perhaps a bold statement of truth, most parents affirm the child's own conclusions—no, Santa is not real. He is make believe.

It is a developmentally significant moment—a child has figured out the difference between fact and fiction, between fantasy and reality, and come to a conclusion based on his or her own thinking process. They see the logical inconsistencies. They reasoned it through.

or cruel deception?(fairy tales can harm the psychology of children). New Scientist 196.2635-2636 (2007).

At this point, you would think a child would be shattered. But studies show that most kids have mixed feelings. They are sad and disappointed but they are also are proud and relieved about having figured it out. Their ideas about reality are confirmed and they no longer need to try to make sense of it. On average, none of the feelings tend to be intense. In other words, they get over it.

Interestingly, parents react more deeply to their child's discovery and tend to be more sad and disappointed than the child. There is the loss of holiday rituals and the fun of keeping it all going. But more importantly, it is a moment when parents realize that their child is maturing. The time of innocence and fantasy has passed. Their baby is growing up.

The Santa Claus myth can have other impacts. Some argue that it encourages children to expect gifts that are given for no reason. Setting aside whether we accept that notion, in the Santa Claus myth, the gift is made as a reward. Santa will not bring presents if a child misbehaves. Parents use Santa as persuasive force.

Even so, none of the stories here mention parents using Santa in that way. Instead, the focus is on parents creating elaborate stories about Santa's behavior so that the child is delayed in figuring it out. Parents tell kids that Santa won't come if they see him or if they are not asleep. In these memoirs, Santa is never one who will exact punishment for misbehavior, but he may disappear if you peek.

Santa Claus also represents a spirit of giving. Kids learn that kindness and giving are what makes Santa special. Santa encourages us to be kind to strangers, and to perhaps keep a little of the sparkle in our own eye when it comes to believing in the goodness of others and ourselves.

We think the following stories will prove that learning the truth about the Santa Claus myth is a moment that each child will find in their own way and that somehow each child will come to terms with the idea that Santa Claus may not be real, but the spirit behind Santa is.

Good-bye, Hello
by
Noëlle Sickels

The January that he turned nine, my son Jude learned there is no Santa Claus. He found a half-used roll of "Santa's" wrapping paper hidden in the back of the linen closet, unhappily drew the logical conclusion, and confirmed its accuracy with a direct question to his father.

Jude came into my bedroom and woke me with the devastating news. He was crying. For days after, at odd moments, he'd make almost bitter, sidelong remarks related to his discovery. "So," he said one day in the car as we were out on errands, "The Easter Bunny and the Tooth Fairy—that's you guys, too, right?" He ruminated over which of his friends might be in the know and which not. Several years earlier, he'd had a heated argument with a Christian Scientist child whose family didn't subscribe to Santa Claus. When the boy's mother had stepped in to support her son's claim that Santa didn't exist, rather than being convinced by her adult authority, Jude was incensed at her ignorance, and his anger at his little friend morphed to pity.

Watching Jude slowly settle into the revised version of his world, I tried to recall my own unseating of Santa at just about the same age. I was the oldest in my family, the first to unmask the fantasy. Thinking back, I conjured up two scenes, both of them in the bathroom. In my childhood home, busy with six children, privacy was a temporary structure designated more by narrowing your scope of attention than by shutting a door. But for me and my mother, the bathroom constituted an inviolate space for serious, private talks.

In the first remembered scene, I am standing in the dark hallway outside the closed bathroom door. It is late on Christmas Eve, and down the hall, my brothers and sisters lie heavily asleep, tangled in sheets and blankets and one another. Earlier in the evening, we'd all carefully chosen long black socks from my father's drawer and laid them out on our beds for Santa to find and fill. From inside the bathroom, I hear rustlings, whispers, even giggles. I open the door, and blinking in the sudden brightness, I see my surprised parents bending over the closed toilet seat lid, on which is piled a jumble of small objects wrapped in aluminum foil. On the edge of the sink rest two lumpy socks, already stuffed with treasures. My father holds another sock, still limp and empty, in his hand.

In the second remembered scene, some days later, my mother reclines Cleopatra-like in the tub. The room is steamy and redolent with Sardo bath oil. She looks at me tenderly, with concern, and asks me what I, many years afterward, will ask my own child. "You sort of knew, didn't you?" Jude will answer, no, he had no idea. I do the same. I sit on that toilet seat lid in the small, humid bathroom and deny any suspicions, deny curiosity, deny my own rational powers.

Of course, somewhere inside me was a weak perception that I had known the facts, but I didn't want to admit it. I wished to be innocent of my own disillusionment. Somehow, I was aware I was relinquishing more than Santa Claus. It was a first step, albeit a small one, outside a protected world, outside the beneficent arms of generous, reliable elves, and complicit, shielding parents. How could I want to take even partial responsibility for such an awesome act?

The step away from Santa was a step toward life on my own; a step toward sex, truth, and death. It was the first edging away from guarantees.

Am I giving my nine—or ten-year-old self too much credit? Yes and no. All these concepts were not there, certainly. But I did feel a sharp trepidation. I sensed significance. And loneliness. Inevitable separations had begun.

I became, with this bit of knowledge, separated at once from my siblings. Now I had to connive to keep the elaborate secret from them. As the oldest, I was used to duties. I pushed the swings, combed out the snarled braids, folded the diapers, fixed the sandwiches, and read the stories. But this was a duty of a different order; one I couldn't beg off or pass on to someone else or forget to do.

There was a shift, too, in my relationship to my parents. In essence, I was inching towards them, towards the adult world, but I felt parted from them. A magical link had been broken. And, in fact, the adulthood on which I was embarking was not theirs, would never be theirs, so I wasn't really joining them, but setting off without them towards some as yet unformed community. Perhaps for the first time, it sank in that I was growing up and that it was an unstoppable process, one that I wasn't sure I was going to like.

In the week after Jude was forced to let go of Santa, I wondered if any such uneasy feelings had been behind his tears and remarks. He certainly was maturing, moving on, and not just because of this. He was still the little boy, affectionate, playful, free with his tears. But I had been seeing him pull in more, too, take painful or difficult situations on his own. And though he would still come to me for comfort, sometimes I had to go to him and press it upon him. He would accept it. It even calmed him some, but there was in his acceptance a politeness, a keeping to ritual, which made me feel he was letting me comfort him for my sake.

He was beginning to see, I think, that his solutions and sorting outs are ultimately on his shoulders. What a lesson to have so young. Yet memory tells me it does begin then, and experience suggests it is begun young because it takes so long to learn.

*   *   *

What to My Wondering Eyes Should Appear
by
John McCluskey

In the last days before Christmas, a flu bug always seemed to slip inside our house and fell one of us mightily. In 1964, it was me. On Christmas Eve, Dad got home from work early, as he did every year, and he took my sister and little brother out for the annual Christmas Eve night drive around the neighborhood to look at all the decorations. Mom always stayed home – for some reason I didn't understand.

I missed it that year, but imagined every minute of the trip: all the way down snowy Drexel Avenue, passed so many houses with lights and glowing Christmas trees in the windows, all misting with the snow. More houses, more lights, until they would get to the house with the complete miniature English snow village set up in the garage. Everything was hand crafted: tiny wooden people, churches, steeples, houses, all of them lit up—the highlight of the ride—joyously displayed every December to great crowds who came from miles away, as the years wore on, while the grownups grumbled, "Good heavens, remember when it was just the neighbors."

We would urge Dad to hurry up after the English village so we could get home. Santa always managed to come to our house Christmas Eve, right when we took our neighborhood drive. When the car pulled into the driveway, we would all hurry out, run through the packed night snow and into the house to be greeted at the door by Mom's every-year surprise at what had happened while we were away. Santa had arrived! "We must be the first ones on his list!" she would announce.

Except this one time. I stayed on the couch, to be close to the tree, in my soupy, dizzy daze, in and out of a fever that could melt the snowdrifts forever away from the side of our house. Cold, then hot, then cold again, I nevertheless felt strangely and sickly comfortable inside the heavy wrap of blankets while the tree energized the room, the night, and the feeling deep within me that this indeed was Christmas Eve, and Dad, my sister, and my brother, would all be back soon, impatient to get home to what was now just moments away. Presents!

Though weak and exhausted, I fought the urge to sleep, excited at first, then panicking that with me here on the couch, how would Santa Claus make it in? And what about Mom? At least she's here every year, surely she knows to stay out of sight; let the jolly old elf work his magic till he'd mush away, the star-like snowy dust from the runners of his sleigh settling softly down with the night flakes on our unsuspecting heads as we would dash in from the cold to see his work.

But maybe I should sleep, let my eyes close to open his way into our house. If I do, he'll come, as he has every year. I closed them tight for as long as I could, and he came to me that year in the form of my mother. Thinking I had finally drifted off for good, she tiptoed down the living room stairs, presents piled high and teetering in arms that hugged me so tender and often during every flu bug battle, and that now, for the first time, threatened to nudge me from the safe couch of childhood, just as I inexplicably decided to open my eyes for a fleeting and endless moment.

She froze on the staircase like the drip-drip-drip from our outside gutter, not entirely certain I had seen her, then tiptoed backwards up the stairs, trusting the wall between us to hide her masquerade and my inevitable fall from the innocence of youth. Delay it once more, her every back-up footstep must have shouted to some distant inner ear of mine, because I then did something that pushed me far closer to shedding my child-skin than finding out no Santa Claus exists would ever do: I kept my eyes closed and pretended to sleep—deeply, protecting my mother from pushing me out of the nest. Don't let her see me knowing the truth. Not yet.

I never moved the whole time she dared return to complete her task. She placed the presents quietly and deliberately in a splendid array beneath the tree just a few feet away. I could smell her perfume and hear her breathing as I continued my own masquerade. I felt my eight-year-old body sink as deep into the couch as it could while she went about her work. Not to hide so much from the disappointment that St. Nick would never again slip through our unguarded doors, more to sink, I suppose, as deeply as possible into the soft and buoyant spirit of a time too soon to be too long gone.

*   *   *

John McCluskey works in the IT industry and lives in Connecticut with his family.

Looking for Santa
by
Valerie Brown-Kuchera

She was beyond beautiful, my newfound best friend. To a farm girl that had never played with other children before this foray into town for kindergarten, this blond, blue-eyed Roxie (who had three cheerleaders as big sisters) was a novelty—a child star. She became, within my first week of school, my muse for all things. Never mind my poor dairywoman mother who put aside every hint of her own desires for her daughter. What could she possibly know about school, clothes, growing up, or math? Roxie, age five, was cosmopolitan.

Roxie had bangs. I trimmed a set for myself, first day home from school. Roxie wore leggings and a colorful belt. I spent my second afternoon home cutting up old shirts with pinking shears, trying to fashion a belt that might pass for store-bought. Roxie chewed with her mouth closed at school lunch. I spent the third evening home from school lecturing my folks about the virtues of table manners (between bites, of course). And finally, on the fourth day of kindergarten lunchtime, my beautiful idol said something that made me pause.

"You know there's no Santa Claus, right?" she asked flippantly.

I masked my surprise by chewing. I put up one finger, a gesture that said, "Just one moment while I finish delicately chewing this dainty bite." I masticated the food and the thought of there not being a Santa Claus simultaneously. Neither was appetizing.

Santa Claus was a big deal at my house. My mom and dad, poor as they were, depended on him to provide Christmas joy. The buildup was the biggest drama of the year for my folks. On Christmas Eve, as my mom was finishing the evening milking, my dad would say mysteriously, "What was that red light beyond the Smith place? Did you see that? I wonder if that could possibly be Rudolph's nose."

This was the signal that the excitement was beginning. I would run to the window, heart beating quickly, but I wouldn't see the light.

"That light bobbed behind a hill. If it is Santa, he must have touched down! Let's take a drive . . . see if we can get a closer look." Dad's infectious air of mystery caught.

Bundling up quickly, we'd run out to the car. And we would drive. Country roads are as dark as they come at 9:00 in December. We hardly ever went anywhere at night, so just being out there in that vast plain was enough to cause my whole body to tingle. But being out there looking for Santa, well, that was enough to bring me near to ecstasy.

Each year, as we sang "Rudolph the Red-Nosed Reindeer" at the top of our lungs, we would crest the same hill. And low and behold, there would be a red light near the roofline of the Smith house. As we came around a bend in the road, the light would disappear and my dad would say, "Good grief! He's gone. We are next on his list! We better go home to bed so he doesn't skip our house!" He would step on the accelerator and our car would race through a darkness that was undeniably filled with magic.

I can hardly describe the breathtaking, almost painful, bliss of my little girl's mind as I ran to the door of our old farmhouse those Christmas Eve nights. Without variation, my mom would be standing there in her milking boots. She would say, "Oh my goodness. As I was walking up from the milk barn, I heard hooves and all kinds of commotion! I looked up and I saw Santa's sleigh taking off from the top of our house! He's been here!"

"Oh no!" Dad would shout. "He probably skipped us since you caught him. He probably didn't have time to leave anything!"

We'd run into the house to find the stockings bulging, the tree surrounded by gifts, and even the smell of peppermint hanging in the air. Chaos was rampant as candy and packaging flew. It was the climax. It was always worth every tense moment of waiting.

So, when beautiful Roxie's lips released such devastating information, I could hardly swallow it. I was Roxie's biggest fan, and I was willing to overlook many a flaw, but this—this blatant disregard for truth—surely it was sacrilegious?

I was hard pressed to chew with my mouth closed much longer, so, as casually as I could, I mustered, "Yeah. I know."

On the long bus ride home from school, I fought the knowledge. I pushed down the memory of the one spring night we'd driven past the Smith place; I saw that same red light near the roofline. I pushed down the realization that it was just too coincidental that Christmas Eve played out exactly the same way every year. I pushed down the nagging thought that the tags on the presents from "Santa" were written in my mom's handwriting. And as the bus pulled to a stop in front of our sagging stoop, I started to hate pretty Roxie, just a little bit.

My mom was already doing the evening milking, so I headed straight to the barn. As I burst into the milking parlor, I said in an accusatory voice, "Roxie says there's no Santa. Is there?"

Mom couldn't hug me because her rubber milking apron was messy and she was wearing thick gloves as well. She said, "Oh honey. Do you promise you won't cry?" That should have been a giant clue to the question's answer, but my five-year old denial was going full force.

"Yes, I promise I won't cry, Mom. Please tell me the truth."

And just like that, it was over. She said, gently, "No, there is no Santa. It's just us. Just mommy and daddy that give you presents."

And disregarding my clean school clothes and my promise of only seconds ago, I sat down on the dirty dairy barn floor, and I cried.

*   *   *

Valerie Brown-Kuchera is a facilitator of gifted education in northwest Kansas. She is the mother of Millicent, Dashiell, and Clementine. Valerie and her husband, Joel, enjoy restoring their Queen Anne Victorian home, traveling, and exercising.

Santa and the Easter Bunny
by
Greg Shannon

I should have arrived on Christmas Eve, just like Santa. Instead, my mother held off delivering me until the day after Christmas, a long and arduous labor she still talks about sixty years later.

The day after Christmas may be one of the worst days to celebrate a birthday, with much of the holiday excitement wearing thin by then and most of the relatives gone home. On Christmas, I would often get a combined BIG Christmas and birthday present—such as a bicycle or golf clubs—and then, on my birthday, the socks and pajamas. My parents did make sure I always had a cake and sometimes a couple of cousins and friends over for the day, including my closest neighbor, Teddy.

Even so, Santa was pretty important to me. I was a quiet and shy country boy growing up in southern Minnesota. Town events, from parades to the beginning of school, generally overwhelmed me. But Santa captured my imagination and hopes, and I would sit on his lap, listening closely, despite my fears. A couple of faded pictures of Santa and me taken at the old Roxy Theater in Winnebago show me perching on the old man's lap, my eyes wide and expectant, my posture tentative, as if I'm about to escape into air.

I wasn't totally gullible about Santa, though. I had standards for my beliefs and childhood fantasies. One Christmas Eve, my grandmother hired a Santa to stop by her house. I knew right away this Santa was not the real thing. Maybe it was the high pitched "HO HO HO," or the lumpy pillow stuffed and skewed under the suit or the cheap costume from boots to hat, but mostly, I think, it was the fake Santa mask. I knew the truth about this skinny Santa imposter, but I still believed in the real one.

It was the spring after my sixth birthday, sometime before Easter, when Teddy came down the quarter mile from his place for an afternoon of play and exploration. We were about the same size, lean and country-sunned, as we didn't spend much time in front of the TV. We rode ponies and bikes, played cowboys and Indians, dug snow caves in zero-degree temperatures, watched the livestock, and occasionally stampeded the sheep.

Teddy was generally the originator of ideas and instigator of our activities. He was the one who once suggested we make a maze in the small field of oats by somersaulting in various directions and patterns in his family's field, much to his later regret. He suggested we build the nine-hole Wiffle ball golf course in his family's pasture, mowing circular areas for greens. And he orchestrated the tunneling through hay bales in our loft, which did not please my parents, who worried we'd fall through the hole in the floor of the loft where Dad pitched hay to the cattle.

On that spring day, the mud in the farmyard was drying up, and we were down by the old corncrib to the east edge of the windbreak, near the abandoned chicken coop and the ancient tin can pile. After we'd finished digging for treasures in the tin can pile, we were checking out the dusty chicken coop when Teddy said, "There is no Santa Claus."

I stopped poking at a lump of straw in the corner, turned, and peered at him through the dim light. "What do you mean?" I asked.

He explained that my mom and dad were responsible for the gifts that were supposedly from Santa. Then he headed home.

I didn't cry or run to the house or shout at Teddy's back that he was a liar. I thought about this news about Santa Claus and decided I needed to go to a source of wisdom. So, I asked my mom directly, "Is there a real Santa Claus?" She replied with a warm smile and a gentle "no," explaining that she and my dad filled those duties in the spirit of Santa. I thoughtfully accepted her explanation, since, deep down, doubts had already crept into my head ever since the fake Santa appeared at my grandparents' house. But this set me thinking. Easter was coming up shortly.

"So, is there an Easter bunny?" I asked.

Again she responded that she and Dad fulfilled those duties too.

"A tooth fairy?"

The same answer.

A few weeks later, I saw the older and wiser Teddy. Feeling confident in my own new wisdom, I declared, "So, you know if there isn't a Santa Claus, there isn't an Easter Bunny either." I twirled a grass stem between my thumb and index finger, and then flicked it to land in the dirt between our feet.

This time it was Teddy who stopped what he was doing, as if he'd just been told he'd been adopted or his parents were getting a divorce. He raised his eyes slowly from the grass stem and studied the matter-of-fact shrug of my shoulders and the truth in the set of my mouth and eyebrows. I could see the tears welling in his eyes and the revelation behind them, and with a quick turn of his feet and his head hung low, he plodded down the gravel county road to his home.

*   *   *

Greg Shannon is an acupuncturist in central Washington State, who also enjoys hiking in the Cascades, photography and when encouraged by his wife Kathi, writing.

The Truth of Santa Claus
by
Susan Beckham Zurenda

In fifth grade, I called Jean Horton my best friend. Mostly what that meant was I followed along with whatever goings on she decided we'd do. On an unusually mild December afternoon as we trudged up the hill in our neighborhood from her house to mine, Jean decided we should lie down in the middle of the street and think about our forthcoming Christmas gifts. The thought exhilarated me. Danger and magic at the same time. We splayed out on our backs in the middle of Westminster Drive and talked about our lists. Jean's top item was a transistor radio and mine was Mindy Mouse.

I worried out loud whether Santa Claus would be able to produce Mindy because she wasn't your ordinary stuffed animal. Her skin was psychedelic and she was clad in a go-go outfit, boots and all. I'd picked her out when my mother took me "window shopping" a week or so before at Bundy's Toyland. Jean turned her head sideways on the pavement and looked at me.

"Of course, you'll get Mindy," she said. "Your mama probably bought her that day."

"My mama didn't buy her," I corrected. "She's on my list for Santa."

"Get up and follow me," Jean commanded. "I'm going to show you something."

"Okay," I agreed. It hadn't been much fun lying in the street anyway. The pavement was hard, and not even one car had passed to give us the opportunity to hop up just in time to save our lives. We rose from the warm pavement, brushing dirt and loose gravel from our behinds.

"We're going to check the attic," Jean announced as we approached my house. Warm as I was from the sun and the pavement, a frozen feeling fell upon me when I realized what she intended to do. I didn't want her to investigate. Of course, I had doubts about Santa. I was ten years old. But they were only doubts. I still had faith in the magic. And without my faith, what would Christmas morning be? Presents only, without the enchantment of a world beyond my own.

"It won't work," I told Jean. "Mama would hear us going into the attic."

"Sure, it will," she insisted. "All we have to do is make sure she's downstairs. Then, we can pull down the attic stairs quietly. If they're not there, we'll find them somewhere else."

"I don't want to," I said, knowing I would do what she said. I was afraid of not gratifying Jean. I didn't want to hear her call me a chicken.

My mother sat at the kitchen table addressing Christmas cards. I remarked we were going upstairs to my room to play Monopoly, and she nodded without looking up. The situation couldn't have been better for Jean.

The attic steps squeaked a little coming down, but of course, Mama was too far away in mind and body to notice. Jean went first. "Look here," she called down. "Here it is."

I had no choice. I clambered up behind her. What I saw were toys on my brother's list. Mindy Mouse was nowhere. I could hardly explain away my brother's Santa's gifts to Jean, but in my head I counted the cousins whose gifts these could be. Illogically, in that moment, I felt both scared and brave. I asked Jean, "So, okay, where do you think *mine* could be?"

"Probably in the car trunk," she said.

"How do you know?" I asked.

"Because they think we won't search in places we don't usually go," she said.

Again, conveniently, my mother's purse lay upstairs on her dresser. I excavated the keys and we crept down the stairs and sneaked out the front door where Mama couldn't see.

When Jean raised the trunk lid, the dazzling green stripes of Mindy's skin and hot pink boots flashed out in the sunlight. I stared. "See," Jean said. "What did I tell you?"

I don't recall anything else that day. Maybe Jean went home soon after, having accomplished her mission. I imagine I wasn't good company to be around at any rate.

On Christmas Eve, when I went to bed, I lay with my hard-bristled hairbrush under my head to stay awake. My parents waited a long time, but finally I heard them talking in the hall. I heard the squeak of the attic stairs descending. My father told my mother he would get the things from the car and meet her in the den. I took the brush out from under my head. In the morning, I slept late. I didn't beg my parents to get out of bed before dawn to examine Santa's empty milk glass and the residue of cookie crumbs, evidence that the supernatural had actually visited us. Entering the den that Christmas morning, I didn't feel my insides quiver in response to the presents from the fat man who couldn't logically fit but somehow did fit down our chimney. My younger brother was zooming Matchbox cars around his new track. Finally, I picked up my mouse and hugged her. For my brother's sake.

Months later, I was visiting my grandmother, rinsing dishes while she washed, when I turned to her and said, "I guess if there isn't a Santa Claus, there isn't Jesus either." It wasn't something I'd been consciously thinking about. I said it almost randomly. My devoted Christian grandmother's hands came up out of the water. She placed them wet on my shoulders. For a moment I thought I saw fear in her face. And then it was gone. Her eyes shone blue crystalline behind their glasses. "Santa is a symbol of what Jesus is," she said.

"But wasn't Santa all about believing? And then finding out he wasn't true?" I asked.

"No," she said. "Santa represents the spirit of giving—of Christmas—that lives in humanity because of Jesus. Santa is a material way for children to embrace the good in the world. You aren't that child any longer. Faith is what you can't see. It's what makes us want to be like Santa because we believe."

* * *

Susan Beckham Zurenda has been teaching English for 32 years and lives in Spartanburg, SC. She currently teaches AP Language and Literature and Reading Strategies at Spartanburg High School. She received a BA in English and an MEd. in English from Converse College. She is married to Wayne and has two grown daughters.

Santa Knocked Off the Throne
by
Suzanne Williams

I was probably in the fourth grade, nine years old, when a visit to Santa Claus tipped me off that there was NO Santa Claus. Grown-ups never leave well enough alone.

I don't know who sponsored the elementary school kids' visit to Santa Claus that year. It might have been the town's Chamber of Commerce—how else to explain Santa Claus' appearance at the local funeral home. It was a big house with a huge double parlor that could handle us all grade by grade. The first and second graders saw him first while we bigger kids waited along the long hallway between the front door and the back parlor. We talked excitedly about what we were going to ask for. Skates and electric trains, dollhouses, and cowboy outfits were big that year. Finally, the fourth graders were allowed into the back room where volunteer moms lined us up for our turns.

There was Santa beyond the arched doorway, seated in a big throne-like red chair flanked by two decorated Christmas trees (real ones, too). Santa's two helpers stood nearby handing out candy canes to the kids as they paraded out confident that this year Santa would bring the desired presents.

At last it was my turn. I walked up the special red carpet to Santa and he helped me up to his lap. He held me on his knee because my nylon winter coat was slippery. Then Santa asked me what I wanted for Christmas. I looked at Santa face-to-face because Mom and Dad always told me to look at the person when you talked to them. As I started to tell him, my heart fell. It was true after all. I had heard rumors, of course, from the Big Kids that there was no Santa Claus, but I still believed—even in fourth grade and nine years old and could go to the movies by myself. The man dressed up in the familiar red suit was my best friend's father, Penny's dad. I knew those bright blue eyes and smile even with all the Santa white hair and bushy eyebrows and beard. I was sitting on Curt Curtis's knee.

Of course, being a big girl, I didn't say anything except recite my list and thank you for the candy cane. I slowly walked home in the snow, thinking about Mr. Curtis and Santa Claus. It was dark when I got home. After taking off my boots, mittens, hat, scarf and winter coat I went into the kitchen where Mom had some cocoa ready.

"How was your visit with Santa Claus," she asked.

"Mom," I replied, "It was Mr. Curtis. There is no Santa Claus."

"Oh, honey," was all she said.

I thought for a minute. "Do I still get presents?"

Christmas morning came and waiting for me to open the box was the one thing I wanted more than anything else—a new pair of figure skates. Only this year, instead of the tag saying from "Santa" it said "Mom and Dad." They were the best Santa Clauses ever.

I never said anything to Mr. Curtis until many years later at a Christmas gathering when I asked him if he remembered the year he played Santa Claus at the funeral parlor. He did. Mr. Curtis is now 90 years old and he still has a merry twinkle in his eye.

*   *   *

Happily retired, Suzanne Williams lives in Arlington, VA with her husband Carl and ferocious calico cat Callie. She dreams of writing the great American novel after she concocts the perfect BBQ sauce.

The Christmas Helicopter—
When Santa Claus Came to Town
by
Sara Etgen-Baker

Inside our home, the Christmas lights twinkled; the tinsel glistened; the ornaments sparkled; and the Christmas tree silently awaited Santa's arrival. I peered out our living room window and noticed that newly fallen snow had blanketed the neighborhood streets. The barren, frost-covered trees shivered like frail skeletons trembling in the blustery winds, and silent icicles hung from the shimmering housetop roofs.

The mercury had dipped well below freezing, so mother wrapped me in my heaviest coat, forced my hands into last year's mittens, and covered my ears with my father's furry ear muffs. When I stepped outside, I watched my warm breath mingle with the crisp, cold air that stung my cheeks. The gentle snow crunched under my boots as we began the one-mile walk from our house to the downtown plaza where Santa was scheduled to arrive.

As I stood in the plaza with the other children, Christmas waved its magic wand over me. So when I looked up in the sky, I was certain that off in the distance I saw Rudolph, heard Santa's sleigh bells jingling, and believed that Santa would arrive shortly. Suddenly though, I glanced above me and discovered that I wasn't hearing sleigh bells at all. Rather, I was hearing the pole-mounted Christmas bells swaying in the wind. I continued to wait, though, in the bone-crunching cold—the kind of cold that wrenches a child's spirit—until I heard an unfamiliar sound approach the crowd of children.

I heard a steady but rhythmic wop-wop, wop-wop sound. Then out of nowhere, a red helicopter emerged from the wintry sky and slowly descended toward us. The propellers beat the cold air into submission until the helicopter gently landed a few feet from me. In disbelief, I watched as Santa turned off the engine, grabbed his bag of toys, disembarked, and headed straight toward me and the other children shouting, "Ho, Ho, Ho! Merry Christmas boys and girls! Hope you've been good this year."

For some reason, Santa's unconventional arrival both shocked and disturbed me and ignited some fiery questions in my mind. So later when I approached Santa, my burning curiosity took on a life of its own. I blurted out, "Where's your sleigh, Santa? Why didn't you ride it into town?"

"Well, little lady . . . it's at the North Pole being repaired."

"What's wrong with your sleigh?" I continued.

"Just some minor repairs . . . nothing for a little girl to worry about," he retorted.

"Who's fixing it?" I further inquired.

"Well, the magical elves are, of course," he curtly replied.

Then logic diluted my childhood naivety, and I quickly formulated some more serious questions: "But I thought elves made toys! Will they really be able to fix your sleigh in time? How will you deliver presents all over the world without it . . . and . . . and," I stammered, "What about Rudolph and all the other reindeer?"

My innocent persistence rendered Santa speechless. He nervously cleared his throat and disapprovingly raised his right eyebrow, which was brown rather than white like his beard. In that instant, the Santa Claus illusion was gone forever.

I cried as I climbed off Santa's lap, and my mother lovingly wrapped me in her arms, wiped away my tears, and said, "You're gonna be okay, sweetie. You're so smart, and I'm proud of you for discovering the truth."

Then, mother got down on her knees, looked me straight in the eyes, and explained, "Santa Claus is a wonderful made up story like the storybooks you read in school. Even though the stories aren't true, you like them any way, right?"

Reluctantly, I said, "Yes," then sniffled back my tears.

"Well," she continued, "sometimes storybook writers make up stories to tell lessons or share something important. The story of Santa Claus is like that. It's made up to tell children about the spirit of kindness and giving—that's what's important. Do you understand, sweetie?"

Her honesty comforted me as I began to acknowledge the nonexistence of Santa Claus. Her forthrightness also allowed me to reconstruct a more mature reality in light of the new evidence I'd witnessed that day. In the end, the day's events actually prepared me for adulthood, for my mother wisely taught me how to maintain a grip on reality independent of the stories I'd eventually hear and the disillusionments I'd experience as an adult.

*   *   *

Sara Etgen-Baker is a retired educator turned freelance writer who writes memoirs and personal narratives. Several of her manuscripts have appeared in Looking Back Magazine and at <u>WomensMemoirs.com</u>. Other stories have appeared in anthologies such as Wisdom Has a Voice and The Heroic Path to Self Discovery.

The Boy Who Nearly Saw Santa
by
Stephen Wade

At Christmas in our house when I was a boy, there were two lots of presents for everyone. Santa left one lot of presents at the end of our beds, while the second batch in the sitting room was from our parents.

On Christmas Eve, our greatest fear was that we wouldn't get to sleep before Santa arrived on the roof of our house. Were this to happen, our father told us, Santa, who knew everything, would take off into the night-sky to other sleeping children. The real Santa, unlike the pretend one in Santa's Grotto at Switzers department store, couldn't risk being seen by anyone. So we went to considerable efforts to avoid this outcome.

Every year, on the night before Christmas, my two brothers and I tried to stay awake until midnight. My older brother reasoned that, that way, we'd be exhausted, fall into a deep sleep, and wake up long after Santa had been and gone. Perfect—at least in theory.

One particular Christmas that stands out is the year Chris de Burgh's *Spaceman* first "came travelling." I had included the L.P. on the list in the letter I'd sent off to the North Pole.

As a way of keeping awake on the night Santa arrived, we talked in the dark about the stuff we had put on our request lists to Santa. Major items, such as new bikes, telescopes, skateboards and skateboard gear, headed the lists. Lower on the list were smaller things such as, records, paints, board games and selection boxes. Our enthusiasm was clearly reflected in the increasing volume of our voices, because Dad came in and told us we were keeping our younger sister awake in the next room.

We resorted to whispering. Soon, my younger brother was asleep, leaving just two of us to keep each other awake. My older brother and I debated highly important issues that all began with "Imagine", or "What if?" Imagine you lived in a caravan. There'd be no chimney for Santa to enter. Or, what if Santa's sleigh crashed into a plane over snowy mountains on his way from the North Pole? Imagine you woke up when Santa was in the room?

The answers were simple. Santa was magic. He could therefore make himself tiny, and the presents, too, and get into a caravan through a letterbox or an open window. Aircraft had radar, my brother said. He was crazy about all things aeronautical. The pilots would be especially alert for Santa and his sleigh on Christmas Eve. But as for the awful possibility of actually waking up while Santa was in the room, we'd sooner have accepted a dare to look behind the freestanding wardrobe with the lights off while alone in the dark.

I prattled on in the same manner for a while, gradually realizing that I was the last of us three brothers awake. Ordinarily my concern would have centered round the countless possible horrors that lurked in every shadow, under the bed or outside the window. But this was Christmas Eve. Monsters, ghosts, and vampires were impossible on such a special night. What terrified me then had to do with being awake when Santa stopped off at our house. And then it happened.

A rustling sound in the landing was the first warning. Santa had arrived. I heard the squeaking of our baby sister's door. I pictured the presents being placed on her bed. Teddies and stuff, I imagined. Jabs of sweat prickled my forehead. And my stomach felt funny. Santa had to know I was awake. Suddenly, I felt the need to go to the bathroom. That would wait.

Maybe Santa was tired and losing his powers, I thought; didn't know I was awake. And what would he do anyway if I did see him? Perhaps it would be his and my secret always?

In my chest something beat madly at the swishing sound of the bedroom door brushing the carpet. This was it. I'd be the first boy ever to see the real Santa. I clenched my eyes shut. Parcels were being left at the end of my brothers' beds. I waited. My turn next. A heavy parcel in crinkly paper touched my toes. Okay! I tried to open my eyes, but couldn't. It was as though they were stitched shut. I was awake and yet my eyes wouldn't open. I felt the thrilling weight of more parcels piling up at the end of my bed. And still my eyes remained sealed—Santa's magic. And when they did finally open, the awakening light brightening the room through the drawn curtains told me it was Christmas morning.

Santa had been and gone.

*　　*　　*

A prize nominee for the PEN/O'Henry Award, 2011, Irish author Steve Wade's fiction has been published widely in print and online. His work has won awards and been placed in prestigious writing competitions, including being shortlisted among five in the Wasafiri Short Story Prize 2011, a nomination for the Hennessy New Irish Writer Prize, and Second Place in the International Biscuit Publishing contest, 2009. His novel 'On Hikers' Hill' was awarded First Prize in the UK abook2read Literary Competition, December 2010—among the final judging panel was the British lyricist sir Tim Rice. 'On Hikers' Hill' is published as an eBook. www.stephenwade.ie

The Wrapping Paper
by
Cristina J. Baptista

If we were related to Santa Claus, how come I never got all the things I asked for each Christmas? We had to be related to him. I had proof right in my hands.

"Mama," I asked, sitting under the Christmas tree we had built from a box. I scooted low, trying not to get hit in the head with Gramma's ugly round ornaments. The shiny green and purple ones. We always hung those toward the bottom and the back. "Do we know Santa Claus?"

Silence. Mama was blowing dust off Papa's collection of little statues for the nativity set. The shepherd and his sheep seemed to be giving her trouble. She picked at something with her chewed fingernails. Then, "Why do you ask that?"

She sounded weird. Had I said something wrong? I shouldn't have asked. I shouldn't even be by the tree. We weren't allowed to open gifts until Uncle Steve and Gramma were here.

I bit my lower lip and chewed and chewed, even though Papa always told me not to: "*Naõ faz eso*! Don't do that," he'd yell in that voice like tumbling pebbles in my mason jar. "You're going to chew a hole right through one day—right through your lip!"

On my lap, I had a wrapped box twice the size of my head. Bright red wrapping paper, with green wreaths with those red-berries you're not supposed to eat, and golden bells. And something else—maybe a teddy bear, but it did not look like any stuffed bear that I owned. Too brown. Eyes too large, like an alien's. And all of mine had big red bows around their necks, not green ones.

"Mama, this package says it's to me from Santa Claus." I held up the box, pointing at the tag. "See?"

Mama's eyes never looked quite so large and dark. She said her father used to call her "Olive Eyes" because hers looked like the black olives we put in a glass "New York Giants" bowl (it was from a gas station) on the table before dinner. Grandpa died before I was born. I wonder what he would have called me. I didn't have my mother's eyes at all.

"Yes, I see that. But why do you think we know Santa? It's Christmas . . . he came down the chimney last night and left that for you. You didn't see him, did you?" She spoke over her shoulder, holding straw (really bits cut from a broom in the garage) from the manger.

I shook my head quickly. "No, but he uses the same wrapping paper as you do."

"How do you know?"

My mother was silly. I pointed to my older brother's present. "Jason's gift is wrapped in the same paper. And the tag says it's from you and Papa." It was Lego blocks. It had to be. I shook the box a few times and it sounded like blocks. I wonder what I could trade Jay for some Legos?

More silence. My mother was never this quiet. I remembered how she liked to say, "what, the cat got your tongue?", when I didn't answer questions fast enough. The cat must've gotten *her* tongue now. I wondered what cat it could be. *My* black and white cat, Patches, wouldn't take tongues. My cat knew how to be good. Santa Claus only gave presents to good little boys and girls. Maybe cats, too.

"Sweetie, Santa Claus had some leftover wrapping paper and he thought a little girl like you would like it. It has bears on it—I know you like teddy bears. Santa knew, too, so he gave me some. But I used it on your brother's gift because all yours were already wrapped."

My mother was so beautiful when she smiled, even if she showed the crossed front teeth she hated. I wasn't used to seeing her smile at all because of them. She really, really hated those teeth. I'm not supposed to say bad words like "hate," but she did!

"Oh. I see! But when did you talk to Santa? When did you SEE him!?" I was excited. No one I knew had ever seen Santa Claus! Did he really wear a red suit that was probably as itchy as my red wool pajamas with those beige feet that now had holes in each big toe? Was his beard snowy white, like Papa always said? *Pai Natal*, my father called him. "It means 'Father Christmas' in Portuguese."

"No, Crissy, Santa left the paper. With a note." She talked fast and to the ceramic sheep. "Last night, when he brought the presents. I found it this morning and wrapped Jason's present, the last one!"

I nodded, smiling, but felt disappointed. I wanted my mother to have seen and heard Santa Claus. What did he sound like? Maybe like the voice on the cartoon with Frosty and Rudolph we watched last night.

My mother began to turn away. She played with the little yellow lambs for the nativity scene. But I had one more question.

"Mama?"

"Yes, Crissy?" She didn't turn around to face me.

"I know where the paper came from. But Mama," I looked at the gift tag on my box once more just to be sure. "How come Santa Claus has the same handwriting as you?"

*   *   *

Cristina J. Baptista is a poet, writer, and educator from Connecticut. After having spent the past seven years in New York City earning a Ph.D. in American Literature from Fordham University, she's returned to her New England roots. Her motto is "write now: apologize later."

My Real Santa Claus
by
Michael Morgan

December is the month all children anticipate throughout the year, because Christmas Eve is when Santa Claus is expected to come down the chimney and deliver presents to all the good boys and girls around the world.

The whole Santa thing began for me as a little squirt, a barely-not-a-baby toddler, able to walk and talk pretty dang good. Now that I could understand the concept of Santa Claus, I was very excited that Christmas was just around the corner. But the neighbor kids just couldn't leave a four year old alone with his beliefs. They just had to tell me that there was no Santa Claus. I was devastated. But Mom told me that we were going to catch Santa on film when he came through the door. Confused at first, because I thought you had to be asleep when Santa arrived, I learned that there are always exceptions to the rule.

On Christmas Eve, my mom set up the video camera and we waited. Suddenly, the front door opened, and a man with a cheery laugh walked into my house. I couldn't believe my eyes! That night I sat on his knee while he played his banjo and sang. Breaking all the rules, Santa thought I had been such a good boy, he chose to hang out with me!

Throughout my childhood, every Christmas was the same. The man I loved so much came to visit. He didn't always come on December 24. Sometimes it was a day or two before Christmas. He explained that he really wanted to see me, but the elves were packing the sleigh, and the reindeer were resting up for the big night. These experiences were very eye opening for me. I learned things about the jolly native of the North Pole that no one else in the entire world ever knew. For example, I learned that Santa really lives in Arizona, because while the North Pole is where he sets up shop, the climate is far too cold for him. I was more than satisfied because this even dismissed the argument that the North Pole is too cold to sustain human life. I learned that Santa had his own "Dixieland Jazz Band." All of his "elves" were there, and I found out that, contrary to popular belief, his elves are over six feet tall!

When I was 11, I was promoted to "honorary elf." Santa had invited us to see him perform at a restaurant, where a friend and I had joined him in singing carols for the customers. We were presented with elf hats with big ears for the occasion. We were having hard financial times that year, and my Mom was worried about having any kind of Christmas. We had already gone to bed when she received a mysterious phone call, telling her to look out on the front porch. There we found over 50 brightly decorated packages, gifts for both of us, as well as all the fixin's for a wonderful Christmas dinner! Somehow this was all done without anyone making a sound!

After Santa left our house, I could always track his location on the NASA Santa Tracker. But I saw the inconsistencies, even then. Santa had told me Rudolph was imaginary, but NASA showed the sleigh being led by a reindeer with a red nose. I chalked it up to government bungling, because my Santa was always right!

As I grew older, I became suspicious. And finally when I was 12, Mom took me to a pizza parlor and broke the news to me. I was formally introduced to Will Stewart and his wife, Pat. Up until then, I had never seen him out of his red suit, and had not really met "Will Stewart." I was devastated to find out! But soon after, I had a realization of a greater truth.

For most kids in the world, Santa Claus is a guy they see at the mall, and not always the same guy. For some kids, their father dressed up in a red suit and pretended to be Santa Claus long enough to hand them a present and leave. When they learned the truth, they really had something to cry about.

My Santa was always the same man, who truly enjoyed spending time with me. Though he also worked in the malls, I was not just a kid in the crowd. When I finally understood this, I knew that nothing had really changed even though I was told Santa did not exist. Maybe that was true for others, but not for me. Unlike other kids who had no relationship with their beloved fat man, my Santa Claus still exists, just as before. He did not evaporate into legend.

For me, "Santa Will" is forever Santa Claus, and though I will no longer receive wrapped toys from him, he will always be the same wonderful, generous man who became such an important part of my childhood. During my childhood years, I never saw him out of the costume, because he was afraid it would make me put two and two together, at too young an age. But I found out that there's not much difference. He is still the wonderful, generous man he has always been. Despite the fact that he no longer wears the Santa costume, he is the same man who treated me so wonderfully, who went above and beyond to be a truly major highlight of my life. I am very grateful to Will Stewart, because while "Santa Claus" may not exist to others, mine still does.

He still plays the banjo and at Christmas, he puts on the red suit and visits the malls to see children who believe. I may even go to the mall to see him, just to wish him a Merry Christmas.

* * *

Nineteen year old Michael Morgan is the author of two published books, Cat-Boy Vs. The Fatal Game Glitch and Cat-Boy Vs. The Mafia Knights, both of which are available on Amazon.com and Barnesandnoble.com. He resides in Glendale, Arizona with his mother, who is also a writer.

The Year Santa Didn't Come
by
Debbra Summers

It was a Christmas I would never forget.

It wasn't the year I got my toy box, handmade by my dad, complete with my name carved into the front and painted green, my favorite color. It wasn't the year I got my new ice skates, complete with furry covers; or even the year I got my first gift from a boy. No. It wasn't the best Christmas of my life. It was the worst. It was the year Santa didn't come to my house. It was the Christmas I found out he didn't go to anyone's house, because there was no Santa Claus. The year was 1966 and I was 11 years old.

"You have to grow up sometime," said my mom. "I mean really, Debbie, think about it. How could one person travel around the entire world in one night let alone deliver presents to every house?"

I sat there, cross-legged on the floor next to the tree, staring at mom's intentionally obvious handwriting on a package addressed to me from Santa. My heart didn't want to believe what my eyes were seeing. I didn't understand. I had tried so hard to be a good girl that year. Wasn't I good enough? Wasn't I on his nice list? Did he check it twice? And why was she telling me *now*?

I never made a fuss about going to bed on Christmas Eve whenever I was told to, no matter how early it was or how excited I was. My sister and I always left out his favorite cookies—peanut butter, criss-crossed with a fork. I made sure his reindeer had fresh carrots complete with green tops. Didn't Santa know that?

Christmas would never be the same again. There would be no reason to go to bed early on Christmas Eve. No reason to bake peanut butter cookies. Where *did* they go anyway? I wanted to run away. Instead, I thanked mom for the present; I don't even remember what it was. I accepted the next one from dad who always played Santa on Christmas morning just as his dad, my papa, did every year at his house for all the cousins on Christmas day.

The following year on Christmas Eve, my sister and I were in bed. She was fast asleep, but I was still awake, staring at the ceiling when I heard a noise above me.

"Dar, Dar. I shook her. Wake up. Wake up! Listen! Do you hear that? It's Santa. He's on the roof. He's at our house!"

"Www . . . What . . . ? Geez, Deb, you know there's no such thing as Santa," she mumbled as she turned away, yanking the covers over her head.

But I knew better. I believed in the magic of Christmas. Taking the streetcar downtown with Granny to Simpson's Department store to see the animated Christmas windows. Going to the Santa Claus parade with thermoses of hot chocolate. Hanging our Christmas stockings that were filled during the night and waiting for us on our breakfast plates. Sharing dinner at the end of the day when we pulled Christmas crackers and wore the hats we found inside. Christmas would be special no matter how old I was.

Many years later, our nine-year-old nephew came to live with my husband and me. Wanting to make his first Christmas with us a memorable one, I shopped, baked, wrapped, and decorated my way into holiday insanity. During one shopping trip, I discovered a leather strap with five large brass bells on it. Sleigh bells perhaps? No. Reindeer bells. Ignoring the price tag I hurried to the checkout. I couldn't wait for Christmas Eve.

It was a Christmas-card Christmas Eve, cold and clear with large, fluffy snowflakes drifting down from a starry, indigo sky, not a breath of wind behind them. Once our nephew was tucked in and sound asleep, we headed to the front porch. Giving the bells a healthy jingle, my husband tossed them onto the front lawn.

The next morning, we watched as our nephew let the dogs out for their morning ritual. Even though he was in his slippers, when he spotted the bells, he ran down the porch steps onto the white blanket of snow covering the front lawn.

Breathless, he came into the kitchen, with the dogs in tow. "Aunt Deb! Uncle Eric! Look what I found, Santa's sleigh bells!"

"I think they just might be Rudolph's," I suggested.

He thought for a moment. "How are we going to get them back to him?"

"You'll have to wait until next year, kiddo. You can leave them for Santa with the milk and cookies. I'm sure he'll be looking out for them at every stop."

Although we no longer have the bells, their magic lives on. They were returned to Santa the following year as planned and went on to be discovered by our grandchildren on Christmas morning the year after that.

As I get ready for each Christmas, wrapping myself up in the wonder of the season, I always take a moment to hope that the magic of Santa comes to your house. I know he's coming to mine.

*   *   *

Debbra is a Virgo who loves water, words and her life in the country in the Northumberland Hills of Ontario. She still hears the reindeer on the roof and always will.

Believing is Seeing

by

April Whitehurst

Every year as the snow begins to blanket the ground, we start to hear whispers and rumblings of that ripe old question, "Do you believe in Santa Claus?" It passes secretly between the mouths of the youngest making its way to the ears of the elders in hopes that some validation of our beliefs will spring forth, leaving the feeling in your heart that can only be described as "OMG!"

In our home, Santa Claus was always on time. On Christmas Eve, he would come flailing through the door laughing and ringing bells. There was no doubt he was very real. He was shaking and jiggling and he would shout through the window at Rudolph telling him to knock off the silliness on the roof. His loud entrance scared me and often sent me into a string of tears. I did not particularly care for his choice of clothing. He looked like a human candy cane.

When I was eight years old, Santa's eyes began to look very familiar. There was no one kin to me who dressed in that manner and his voice did not match that of anyone I had ever spoken with. However, there was something very comforting about Santa Claus. That year, I felt no fear and the tears did not come. Instead, they were replaced with a huge warm hug from the red and white clad chubby man. Those eyes belonged to my father. He saw the familiarity pass between us and I am sure at that point he knew the question I asked myself every year had been answered. My father was Santa Claus! So he sat me down and explained that Santa Claus needed helpers to share the workload to make sure that everyone would get something. That was the reason there are so many Santa Claus spotted during the holiday season. Once again, he did not confirm or deny his true status as Santa Claus and the same old question lingered in my mind, "Do I believe?"

As my teenage years approached, I began to help my dad every year with his duties as Santa Claus. I became his elf, clad in ridiculous clothes. I had spent my whole childhood laughing at the human candy cane and now I was his sidekick.

Every Christmas Eve, Dad and I would approach a home in desperate need. He would proceed to throw the door open all while bellowing "Merry Christmas!" and shaking a huge set of jingle bells. I was nervous for the people we visited as the human candy cane danced around throwing packages all over the home. The children would come running with absolute joy that Santa had remembered them this year. I knew exactly how they felt. It did not matter what he had for them, it was something, and that meant he had not forgotten them.

I soon grew up and, even as an adult, I was Dad's elf. One snowy Christmas Eve, we were in a department store bringing Christmas cheer. As the ten-hour day passed, we both grew very tired. The children were getting cranky and the parents even worse because they found themselves in a department store on Christmas Eve finishing their last minute shopping. We looked at each other knowing we only had just a few more minutes and the evening would come to an end until the next year.

A woman, perhaps in her late sixties, approached Dad. She had a look of concern on her face. She softly said, "I know you didn't mean to forget about me last year. I am sure you just got busy. If you have time this year Santa, I could use a housecoat and pair of slippers." Dad and I looked at each other in disbelief. Did we hear her right? How could she not have gotten the answer like all of the other children growing up? She believed Dad was Santa Claus!

Dad looked back at the lady and explained, "Yes, my schedule got completely fouled up last year and I do apologize. You can rest assure you will have the finest housecoat and slippers that Santa can get his elves to sew. Elf! Tell the other elves to get cranking on it!" I acknowledged my duty as chief elf to have my staff begin preparing the items Santa Claus had requested. The lady was so grateful she began to cry, as did Santa and the elf. Was this happening? Did she really believe?

As she disappeared down the aisle, Dad looked at me and said, "I have no idea who she is, but I have to find out." At that moment, the answer I had been looking for my whole life was finally given to me as I watched Santa Claus run down the aisle grabbing several house coats, slippers, and gift bags. Making his way to the checkout line, everyone naturally insisted he go first. In full regalia, Santa Claus checked out and followed the lady home to leave her gifts in the pretty Christmas bags on her porch for Christmas Day. Santa did not forget her that year.

As the snowball fights begin and the homes begin to take on the smell of cinnamon each year, the question from my childhood whispers across the lips of young ones giving elders a reason to pause and smile. Do you believe in Santa Claus? I know what I saw in that department store. While everyone else was busy buying for their friends and loved ones, a rotund man dressed like a human candy cane made sure a woman, who believed in him, woke up Christmas morning to find house coats and slippers to make up for the years when she had been forgotten.

*   *   *

April Whitehurst is a full-time student and writer living in Christiansburg, Virginia, with her three sons. She is pursuing a doctorate in Criminal Justice/Psychology to help local law enforcement and various rescue agencies in a counseling capacity to cope with the daily stressors that invade their personal lives.

Printed in the United States
By Bookmasters